THE MAP & THE MIRRORS
THE ALCHEMIST
GUIDE TO
TAROT

BRINGING SIMPLICITY TO THE 78 CARDS
A TRAUMA SURVIVORS JOURNEY THROUGH
TAROT, HEALING & SPIRITUAL REBIRTH

BY: ASHTON
ASHCROFT

Preface

I didn't write this book to impress anyone. I wrote it to make Tarot feel more personal, more accessible & less like a language you need permission to speak.

This is not an overly complicated guide. I kept it simple on purpose. Each card holds space for its own voice without too much filler or fluff.

You'll find keywords, core energy, upright & reversed meanings & some basic associations like zodiac signs, but what matters most is what you hear when you look at the card.

I centered the text & left margins wide on both sides so you can scribe your own meanings, stories & experiences as you go.

My hope is that this book becomes a conversation between you & the cards, not a script you have to follow.

Let them speak.

Then write back.

WHY THIS BOOK EXISTS

I'VE LIVED THROUGH THINGS THAT TORE HOLES IN THE STORY I THOUGHT MY LIFE WOULD BE. GRIEF THAT NEVER LEFT.

LOVE THAT HURT. A BODY MARKED BY BOTH SURVIVAL & STIGMA. SILENCE THAT NEARLY SWALLOWED ME.

THERE WERE TIMES I DIDN'T HAVE WORDS FOR WHAT I FELT. TAROT GAVE ME THOSE WORDS.

THE CARDS DIDN'T SAVE ME, BUT THEY SAW ME. THEY NAMED THINGS I COULDN'T. THEY HELPED ME LOOK AT WHAT I WAS AFRAID TO FACE & GAVE ME SYMBOLS TO HOLD ONTO WHEN EVERYTHING ELSE FELL APART.

TAROT HELPED ME MAKE MEANING OUT OF MOMENTS THAT FELT SENSELESS. IT GAVE SHAPE TO THE CHAOS. SOMETIMES, IT JUST GAVE ME PERMISSION TO FEEL WITHOUT NEEDING TO FIX IT.

THIS BOOK ISN'T ABOUT "LEARNING TAROT THE RIGHT WAY." IT'S ABOUT RECLAIMING YOUR WAY OF LISTENING. I WROTE IT AS SOMEONE WHO KNOWS WHAT IT'S LIKE TO SEARCH FOR CLARITY IN THE DARK.

YOU'LL FIND STRUCTURE HERE, BUT ALSO SPACE. ROOM FOR THE CARDS TO SPEAK & FOR YOU TO ANSWER HONESTLY.

IF YOU'VE EVER FELT LIKE YOUR STORY DIDN'T MAKE SENSE, OR LIKE NO ONE GAVE YOU THE TOOLS TO TELL IT, LET THIS BE A BEGINNING.

A MIRROR.

A MOMENT OF STILLNESS.

A WAY THROUGH.

Dedicated to you

For the ones who survived what should have broken them.

For the quiet healers, the misfits, the feelers, the forgotten.

For every time you picked up the pieces & called it a ritual.

For the version of me that didn't think they'd make it this far.

This is for you.

This is for us.

I am because I feel, I do because I love.

I speak into existence, so that I may see the world unfold before me.

I am that I feel & I feel that I am.

So that I know, that I am.

How To Use This
Book

This book isn't meant to be read cover to cover.

It's meant to be returned to, flipped open when you need insight, affirmation, or a different way to see something.

Use it like a mirror, a journal companion, or a study guide.

Each page has space around it for a reason.

Let the cards speak to you, then write down what they say.

Let your intuition fill in the blanks.

Let this book grow with you.

When the meanings don't make sense, sit with them anyway.

You're not wrong.

You're just in your own story & that's the only one that matters here.

Major Arcana

The Major Arcana is the heart of the Tarot.

It's made up of 22 cards, each showing a key stage in what's often called the "Fool's Journey" a symbolic path of growth from innocence to self-awareness.

Think of It As:

A map of the soul's growth, a mirror reflecting your spiritual evolution, a sequence where each card is a threshold or milestone in consciousness.

Cards 0–7: Conscious self

Cards 8–14: Challenge or shadow

Cards 15–21: Spiritual integration

What They Represent:

Big themes: Life-changing moments, spiritual lessons, karmic cycles

Depth: More than daily events, these cards signal turning points

Function: They frame the reading with meaning beyond the mundane

0 - The Fool (Uranus) - 0
Innocence, potential, the leap
Upright: New beginnings, risk, potential
Reversed: Recklessness, naivety, inconsistency

1 - The Magician (Mercury) - I
Willpower, action, manifestation
Upright: Manifestation, skill, action
Reversed: Manipulation, poor planning, illusions

2 - The High Priestess (Moon) - II
Intuition, mystery, inner knowing
Upright: Intuition, secrets, subconscious
Reversed: Secrets, hidden agendas, disconnected

3 - The Empress (Venus) - III
Nurturing, creativity, nature
Upright: Fertility, creation, nurture
Reversed: Dependency, smothering, creative block

4 - The Emperor (Aries) - IV
Structure, authority, foundation
Upright: Authority, stability, leadership
Reversed: Domination, rigidity, inflexibility

5 - The Hierophant (Taurus) - V
Tradition, learning, systems
Upright: Tradition, wisdom, structure
Reversed: Rebellion, ignorance, unconventional

6 - The Lovers (Gemini) - VI
Choice, union, duality
Upright: Union, choices, harmony
Reversed: Disharmony, imbalance, misalignment

7 - The Chariot (Cancer) - VII
Will, discipline, focused intent
Upright: Willpower, control, victory
Reversed: Lack of control, aggression, defeat

8 - Strength (Leo) - VIII
Courage, inner calm, patience
Upright: Courage, patience, inner strength
Reversed: Weakness, self-doubt, insecurity

9 - The Hermit (Virgo) - IX
Solitude, wisdom, reflection
Upright: Reflection, solitude, guidance
Reversed: Isolation, loneliness, withdrawal

10 - Wheel of Fortune (Jupiter) - X
Fate, cycles, change
Upright: Cycles, fate, change
Reversed: Bad luck, resistance to change, setbacks

11 - Justice (Libra) - XI
Truth, fairness, cause & effect
Upright: Truth, balance, fairness
Reversed: Injustice, dishonesty, imbalance

12 - The Hanged Man (Neptune) - XII
Surrender, perspective, pause
Upright: Surrender, new perspective, pause
Reversed: Stalling, indecision, martyrdom

13 - Death (Scorpio) - XIII
Endings, transformation, letting go
Upright: Transformation, endings, rebirth
Reversed: Resistance, stagnation, fear of change

21 - THE WORLD (SATURN) - XXI
COMPLETION, INTEGRATION, WHOLENESS
UPRIGHT: COMPLETION, ACHIEVEMENT, TRAVEL
REVERSED: LACK OF CLOSURE, INCOMPLETION, SHORTCUTS

Wands

Element: Fire

Signs: Aries, Leo, Sagittarius

Birthdates:

Aries: March 21-April 19

Leo: July 23-August 22

Sagittarius: November 22-December 21

Theme: Drive, spirit, creativity

Focus: Passion, ambition, action, inspiration, purpose

Energy: Dynamic, bold, initiating

Shadow side: Impulsiveness, burnout, arrogance

1 of Wands - I
Upright: Beginnings, spark, potential
Reversed: Blocked, distorted, or excessive beginnings, spark, potential

2 of Wands - II
Upright: Balance, duality, partnership
Reversed: Blocked, distorted, or excessive balance, duality, partnership

3 of Wands - III
Upright: Growth, creation, teamwork
Reversed: Blocked, distorted, or excessive growth, creation, teamwork

4 of Wands - IV
Upright: Stability, structure, rest
Reversed: Blocked, distorted, or excessive stability, structure, rest

5 of Wands - V
Upright: Conflict, change, struggle
Reversed: Blocked, distorted, or excessive conflict, change, struggle

6 of Wands - VI
Upright: Harmony, movement, generosity
Reversed: Blocked, distorted, or excessive harmony, movement, generosity

7 of Wands - VII
Upright: Challenges, strategy, endurance
Reversed: Blocked, distorted, or excessive challenges, strategy, endurance

8 of Wands - VIII
Upright: Mastery, action, progress
Reversed: Blocked, distorted, or excessive mastery, action, progress

9 of Wands - IX
Upright: Fulfillment, anxiety, resilience
Reversed: Blocked, distorted, or excessive fulfillment, anxiety, resilience

10 of Wands - X
Upright: Completion, burden, culmination
Reversed: Blocked, distorted, or excessive completion, burden, culmination

Page of Wands:
Upright: Curiosity, message, exploration
Reversed: Blocked, distorted, or excessive curiosity, message, exploration

Knight of Wands:
Upright: Pursuit, ambition, energy
Reversed: Blocked, distorted, or excessive pursuit, ambition, energy

Queen of Wands:
Upright: Nurturing, influence, intuition
Reversed: Blocked, distorted, or excessive nurturing, influence, intuition

King of Wands:
Upright: Authority, mastery, leadership
Reversed: Blocked, distorted, or excessive authority, mastery, leadership

Cups

Element: Water

Signs: Cancer, Scorpio, Pisces

Birthdates:

Cancer: June 21- July 22

Scorpio: October 23-November 21

Pisces: February 19-March22

Theme: Emotions, relationships, connection

Focus: Love, intuition, healing, compassion, the
heart & soul

Energy: Fluid, sensitive, receptive

Shadow side: Emotional overwhelm, fantasy,
codependence

1 of Cups - I
UPRIGHT: BEGINNINGS, SPARK, POTENTIAL
REVERSED: BLOCKED, DISTORTED, OR EXCESSIVE BEGINNINGS, SPARK, POTENTIAL

2 of Cups - II
UPRIGHT: BALANCE, DUALITY, PARTNERSHIP
REVERSED: BLOCKED, DISTORTED, OR EXCESSIVE BALANCE, DUALITY, PARTNERSHIP

3 of Cups - III
UPRIGHT: GROWTH, CREATION, TEAMWORK
REVERSED: BLOCKED, DISTORTED, OR EXCESSIVE GROWTH, CREATION, TEAMWORK

4 of Cups - IV
UPRIGHT: STABILITY, STRUCTURE, REST
REVERSED: BLOCKED, DISTORTED, OR EXCESSIVE STABILITY, STRUCTURE, REST

5 of Cups - V
UPRIGHT: CONFLICT, CHANGE, STRUGGLE
REVERSED: BLOCKED, DISTORTED, OR EXCESSIVE CONFLICT, CHANGE, STRUGGLE

6 of Cups - VI
UPRIGHT: HARMONY, MOVEMENT, GENEROSITY
REVERSED: BLOCKED, DISTORTED, OR EXCESSIVE HARMONY, MOVEMENT, GENEROSITY

7 of Cups - VII
UPRIGHT: CHALLENGES, STRATEGY, ENDURANCE
REVERSED: BLOCKED, DISTORTED, OR EXCESSIVE CHALLENGES, STRATEGY, ENDURANCE

8 of Cups - VIII
UPRIGHT: MASTERY, ACTION, PROGRESS
REVERSED: BLOCKED, DISTORTED, OR EXCESSIVE MASTERY, ACTION, PROGRESS

9 of Cups - IX
UPRIGHT: FULFILLMENT, ANXIETY, RESILIENCE
REVERSED: BLOCKED, DISTORTED, OR EXCESSIVE FULFILLMENT, ANXIETY, RESILIENCE

10 of Cups - X
UPRIGHT: COMPLETION, BURDEN, CULMINATION
REVERSED: BLOCKED, DISTORTED, OR EXCESSIVE COMPLETION, BURDEN, CULMINATION

PAGE OF CUPS:
UPRIGHT: CURIOSITY, MESSAGE, EXPLORATION
REVERSED: BLOCKED, DISTORTED, OR EXCESSIVE CURIOSITY, MESSAGE, EXPLORATION

KNIGHT OF CUPS:
UPRIGHT: PURSUIT, AMBITION, ENERGY
REVERSED: BLOCKED, DISTORTED, OR EXCESSIVE PURSUIT, AMBITION, ENERGY

QUEEN OF CUPS:
UPRIGHT: NURTURING, INFLUENCE, INTUITION
REVERSED: BLOCKED, DISTORTED, OR EXCESSIVE NURTURING, INFLUENCE, INTUITION

KING OF CUPS:
UPRIGHT: AUTHORITY, MASTERY, LEADERSHIP
REVERSED: BLOCKED, DISTORTED, OR EXCESSIVE AUTHORITY, MASTERY, LEADERSHIP

Swords

Element: Air

Signs: Gemini, Libra, Aquarius

Birthdates:

Gemini: May 21-June 20

Libra: September 23-October 22

Aquarius: January 20-February 18

Theme: Thought, conflict, truth

Focus: The mind, logic, communication, decision-making & sometimes internal or external battles

Energy: Sharp, fast, often intense

Shadow side: Anxiety, harsh words, overthinking

1 of Swords - I
Upright: Beginnings, spark, potential
Reversed: Blocked, distorted, or excessive beginnings, spark, potential

2 of Swords - II
Upright: Balance, duality, partnership
Reversed: Blocked, distorted, or excessive balance, duality, partnership

3 of Swords - III
Upright: Growth, creation, teamwork
Reversed: Blocked, distorted, or excessive growth, creation, teamwork

4 of Swords - IV
Upright: Stability, structure, rest
Reversed: Blocked, distorted, or excessive stability, structure, rest

5 of Swords - V
Upright: Conflict, change, struggle
Reversed: Blocked, distorted, or excessive conflict, change, struggle

6 of Swords - VI
Upright: Harmony, movement, generosity
Reversed: Blocked, distorted, or excessive harmony, movement, generosity

7 of Swords - VII
Upright: Challenges, strategy, endurance
Reversed: Blocked, distorted, or excessive challenges, strategy, endurance

8 of Swords - VIII
Upright: Mastery, action, progress
Reversed: Blocked, distorted, or excessive mastery, action, progress

9 of Swords - IX
Upright: Fulfillment, anxiety, resilience
Reversed: Blocked, distorted, or excessive fulfillment, anxiety, resilience

10 of Swords - X
Upright: Completion, burden, culmination
Reversed: Blocked, distorted, or excessive completion, burden, culmination

Page of Swords:
Upright: Curiosity, message, exploration
Reversed: Blocked, distorted, or excessive curiosity, message, exploration

Knight of Swords:
Upright: Pursuit, ambition, energy
Reversed: Blocked, distorted, or excessive pursuit, ambition, energy

Queen of Swords:
Upright: Nurturing, influence, intuition
Reversed: Blocked, distorted, or excessive nurturing, influence, intuition

King of Swords:
Upright: Authority, mastery, leadership
Reversed: Blocked, distorted, or excessive authority, mastery, leadership

Pentacles

Element: Earth

Signs: Taurus, Virgo, Capricorn

Birthdates:

Taurus: April 20-May 20

Virgo: August 23-September 22

Capricorn: December 22-January 19

Theme: The physical world, material matters

Focus: Career, money, health, home, long-term effort

Energy: Grounded, steady, practical

Shadow side: Greed, stagnation, insecurity

1 of Pentacles - I
UPRIGHT: Beginnings, spark, potential
REVERSED: Blocked, distorted, or excessive beginnings, spark, potential

2 of Pentacles - II
UPRIGHT: Balance, duality, partnership
REVERSED: Excessive balance, duality, partnership

3 of Pentacles - III
UPRIGHT: Growth, creation, teamwork
REVERSED: Blocked, distorted, or excessive growth, creation, teamwork

4 of Pentacles - IV
UPRIGHT: Stability, structure, rest
REVERSED: Blocked, distorted, or excessive stability, structure, rest

5 of Pentacles - V
UPRIGHT: Conflict, change, struggle
REVERSED: Blocked, distorted, or excessive conflict, change, struggle

6 of Pentacles - VI
UPRIGHT: Harmony, movement, generosity
REVERSED: Blocked, distorted, or excessive harmony, movement, generosity

7 of Pentacles - VII
UPRIGHT: Challenges, strategy, endurance
REVERSED: Blocked, distorted, or excessive challenges, strategy, endurance

8 of Pentacles - VIII
UPRIGHT: MASTERY, ACTION, PROGRESS
REVERSED: BLOCKED, DISTORTED, OR EXCESSIVE MASTERY, ACTION, PROGRESS

9 of Pentacles - IX
UPRIGHT: FULFILLMENT, ANXIETY, RESILIENCE
REVERSED: BLOCKED, DISTORTED, OR EXCESSIVE FULFILLMENT, ANXIETY, RESILIENCE

10 of Pentacles - X
UPRIGHT: COMPLETION, BURDEN, CULMINATION
REVERSED: BLOCKED, DISTORTED, OR EXCESSIVE COMPLETION, BURDEN, CULMINATION

Page of Pentacles:
UPRIGHT: CURIOSITY, MESSAGE, EXPLORATION
REVERSED: BLOCKED, DISTORTED, OR EXCESSIVE CURIOSITY, MESSAGE, EXPLORATION

Knight of Pentacles:
UPRIGHT: PURSUIT, AMBITION, ENERGY
REVERSED: BLOCKED, DISTORTED, OR EXCESSIVE PURSUIT, AMBITION, ENERGY

Queen of Pentacles:
UPRIGHT: NURTURING, INFLUENCE, INTUITION
REVERSED: BLOCKED, DISTORTED, OR EXCESSIVE NURTURING, INFLUENCE, INTUITION

King of Pentacles:
UPRIGHT: AUTHORITY, MASTERY, LEADERSHIP
REVERSED: BLOCKED, DISTORTED, OR EXCESSIVE AUTHORITY, MASTERY, LEADERSHIP

Groupings & Their Meanings in Your Spread:

When multiple cards with the same number appear in a reading, like several Twos, Threes, Fours etc.

It adds a layer of meaning beyond the individual cards.

While each card still holds its traditional message, the repetition of a number pattern points to a deeper theme unfolding across the spread.

These number groupings can signal energetic patterns, emotional climates, or stages of a process.

They act like echoes, reinforcing a particular frequency or challenge that's present.

ACES:

FOUR: A TIME OF NEW BEGINNINGS, LOTS OF ENERGY & POTENTIAL
THREE: GOOD NEWS ON ITS WAY
TWO: A NEW HOME OR LOVE AFFAIR

TWOS - II

FOUR: GATHERINGS OF PEOPLE
THREE: MANY CHANGES ON HORIZON
TWO: AT A CROSSROADS, IMPORTANT DECISIONS UPCOMING

THREES - III

FOUR: A CALL FOR CREATIVITY & DETERMINATION
THREE: POSSIBLE DECEIT, CHANGE IN CIRCUMSTANCES
TWO: PROGRESS THROUGH COLLABORATION

FOURS - IV

FOUR: CONTENTMENT & SECURITY IN ONES SELF OR THE SITUATION
THREE: HARD WORK & ENDURANCE REQUIRED
TWO: A NEED TO PAUSE & REASSESS

FIVES - V

FOUR: COMPETITION & DISCORD
THREE: A NEED TO ESTABLISH A ROUTINE & ACTIVES.
TWO: GROWTH IS POSSIBLE, BUT ONLY THROUGH FACING THE DISCOMFORT

SIXES - VI

FOUR: GOOD FELLOWSHIP & HARMONY AHEAD
THREE: ACKNOWLEDGEMENT OF ONES OWN ACHIEVEMENTS
TWO: A NEED FOR EQUAL GIVE & TAKE

Sevens - VII

Four: Intrigue, lies, theft
Three: Good Fortune is on the horizon
Two: A test of ones faith or trust

Eights - VIII

Four: Upcoming journeys or travel
Three: Good news in regards to a relationship
Two: A new level of responsibility

Nines - IX

Four: High achievements, rewards, or awards
Three: Good health & prosperity
Two: Close to completing a cycle, stay grounded

Tens - X

Four: Remarkable triumph, overcoming obstacles
Three: Legal problems
Two: Carrying to many burdens

Pages:

Four: Schooling, college, university
Three: Good fun, social life, parties
Two: Quarrels between friends

Knights:

Four: Quick action is needed
Three: A small gathering of men
Two: Reunion with old friends

QUEENS:

FOUR: A SMALL GATHERING OF WOMEN
THREE: HELPFUL FEMALE FRIENDS
TWO: GOSSIP, BACKSTABBING, RIVALRY

KINGS:

FOUR: HIGH ACHIEVEMENTS, IMPORTANT AFFAIRS, RECOGNITION BY PEERS
THREE: A GATHERING OF POWERFUL & INFLUENTIAL MEN
TWO: A NEW BUSINESS PARTNERSHIP OR COOPERATION

TAROT WITH PLAYING CARDS

YOU DON'T NEED A TRADITIONAL TAROT DECK YO BEGIN READING CARDS. A STANDARD DECK OF PLAYING CARDS, 52 CARDS WITH HEARTS, DIAMONDS, CLUBS & SPADES, CAN SERVE AS A POWERFUL ALTERNATIVE.

WHILE IT DOES NOT INCLUDE THE 22 MAJOR ARCANA CARDS, THE STRUCTURE OF THE MINOR ARCANA IS ALREADY BUILT IN. EACH SUIT IN A REGULAR DECK MIRRORS ONE OF THE FOUR TAROT SUITS: HEARTS ARE CUPS, DIAMONDS ARE PENTACLES, CLUBS ARE WANDS & SPADES ARE SWORDS.

HEARTS TAP INTO LOVE, EMOTION & CONNECTION. DIAMONDS DEAL WITH THE MATERIAL WORLD, MONEY, HEALTH & WORK. CLUBS CARRY THE FIRE OF CREATIVITY, DRIVE & PERSONAL WILL. SPADES CUT THROUGH THOUGHT, TRUTH, CONFLICT & SHADOW.

THE COURT CARDS ARE EASY TO TRANSLATE AS WELL: THE JACK IS YOUR PAGE, THE QUEEN & KING REMAIN THE SAME, SOME READERS WILL INTERPRET THE JOKERS AS A PLACEHOLDER FOR DEEPER SYMBOLIC ENERGY.

WHILE A STANDARD DECK WON'T GIVE YOU THE MYTHIC ARCHITECTURE OF THE MAJOR ARCANA, ITS STILL A RICH TOOL FOR INSIGHT, REFLECTION & STORYTELLING, ESPECIALLY WHEN YOU LEARN TO LISTEN THROUGH THE SUITS THEMSELVES.

IF ANYTHING, IT REMINDS YOU THAT IT'S NOT THE DECK THAT GIVES YOU THE READING POWER.

IT IS YOUR PRESENCE WITH IT.

READERS REFLECTIONS

WHAT DID I LEARNED FROM MY SPREAD?

WHAT CARDS KEPT SHOWING UP?

WHAT TRUTH AM I AVOIDING?

Readers Reflections

Where do I Need more clarity?

What memories came to mind when doing my spread?

What lesson am I resisting?

Readers Reflections

Who in my life is this reading for?

What truth was I invited to face today?

What part of my life needs attention?

READERS REFLECTIONS

HOW CAN I CHANGE THE PRESENT TO POSITIVELY AFFECT MY FUTURE?

WHAT DO I NEED TO RELEASE IN MY LIFE IN MY LIFE?

WHERE IN MY BODY DID I FEEL THIS READING?

Readers Reflections

What part of your energy haven't you fully understood yet?

What colors, sounds, feeling, or emotions rose in your body during your reading?

Readers Reflections

What small step was I invited to take today?

If these cards could speak to you, what would they say today?

Based off your reading today, how would courage look for you?

A FAREWELL TO YOU

TAROT DIDN'T GIVE ME ALL THE ANSWERS.

IT JUST REMINDED ME I WAS ALLOWED TO ASK THE QUESTIONS.

IF YOU'VE MADE IT TO THE END OF THIS BOOK, THEN MAYBE
YOU'VE STARTED ASKING YOUR OWN.

KEEP GOING.

LET THE CARDS SPEAK WHEN YOU CAN'T.

LET YOUR STORY SHIFT & CHANGE.

LET YOUR TRUTH BE FLUID, LIKE INK, LIKE WATER, LIKE
BREATH.

WHEN YOU NEED TO, COME BACK TO THE BEGINNING.

START AGAIN.

I AM BECAUSE I FEEL, I DO BECAUSE I LOVE.

I SPEAK INTO EXISTENCE, SO THAT I MAY SEE THE WORLD
UNFOLD BEFORE ME.

I AM THAT I FEEL & I FEEL THAT I AM,
SO THAT I KNOW, THAT I AM.